Time Management

Get an extra day a week

Fourth Edition

Marion E. Haynes

50-Minute Manager™

This 50-Minute Manager™ book is designed to be an excellent workbook for self-study as well as classroom learning. All material is copyright-protected and cannot be duplicated without permission from the publisher. *Therefore, be sure to order a copy for every training participant through our Web site, 50minutemanager.com.*

Time Management

Get an extra day a week

Fourth Edition

Marion E. Haynes

CREDITS:

President, Axzo Press: **Jon Winder**
Vice President, Product Development: **Charles G. Blum**
Vice President, Operations: **Josh Pincus**
Director, Publishing Systems Development: **Dan Quackenbush**
Copy Editor: **Ken Maher**

For more information, go to www.logicaloperations.com

Printed in the United States of America
1 2 3 4 5 08 07 06

Table of Contents

About the Author

Marion E. Haynes is the author of three titles in the Crisp 50-Minute Series. He has published 35 articles and ten books on management and supervisory practices, as well as retirement and life planning.

Mr. Haynes is a graduate of Arizona State University with a BS degree in Business Administration. He holds the MBA degree, with distinction, from New York University.

He retired from Shell Oil Company in 1991 after a 35-year career in human resource management. At retirement, he was the corporate level manager of pensioner relations. Following retirement, he joined the staff of Price-Waterhouse as a consultant working as a member of a three-person team presenting retirement planning workshops for Price-Waterhouse clients.

Mr. Haynes was appointed an adjunct professor at the University of Houston's College of Continuing Education. He also served as an instructor for the hospitality industry's executive course presented each year by the University's Conrad Hilton College of Hotel and Restaurant Management. He also presented public workshops at several universities in the South-Central U.S.

He served for four years on the board of directors of Sheltering Arms, a social service agency for the elderly in Houston, Texas. During this time, he chaired the agency's personnel committee and served on its executive committee.

He was a member of the board of directors of the International Society for Retirement Planning for eight years, serving as president from 1991 to 1993. He also chaired the editorial board for the society's journal and served on its newsletter board.

Today, he and his wife, Janice, live in Kerrville, Texas, where he pursues his interests in writing, community service, and travel.

Preface: The Tyranny of the Urgent

Have you ever wished for a thirty-hour day? Surely this extra time would relieve the tremendous pressure under which we live. Our lives leave a trail of unfinished tasks. Unanswered letters, unvisited friends, unwritten articles, and unread books haunt quiet moments when we stop to evaluate.

But would a thirty-hour day really solve the problem? Wouldn't we soon be just as frustrated as we are now with our twenty-four allotment? A mother's work is never finished, and neither is that of any manager, student, teacher, or anyone else we know.

When we stop to evaluate, we realize that our dilemma goes deeper than shortage of time; it's basically the problem of priorities. Hard work doesn't hurt us. We know what it is to go full speed for long hours, and the resulting weariness is matched by a sense of achievement. Not hard work, but doubt and misgiving produce anxiety as we review a month or year and become oppressed by the pile of unfinished tasks. Demands have driven us onto a reef of frustration. We confess, quite apart from our sins, "we have left undone those things which we ought to have done; and we have done those things which we ought not to have done."

Several years ago, an experienced manager said to me, "Your greatest danger is letting the urgent things crowd out the important." He didn't realize how hard his maxim hit. It often returns to haunt and rebuke me by raising the critical problem of priorities.

We live in constant tension between the urgent and the important. The problem is that the important task rarely must be done today, or even this week. The urgent task calls for instant action—endless demands, pressure every hour and day.

Even a home is no longer a castle; no longer a place away from urgent tasks, because the telephone breaches the walls with imperious demands. The momentary appeal of new distractions seems irresistible and important, and they devour our energy. But in the light of time's perspective, their deceptive prominence fades; and with a sense of loss, we recall important tasks we have pushed aside. We realize we've become slaves to the "tyranny of the urgent."

Edited from Tyranny of the Urgent, *by Dr. Charles E. Hummell (Downers Grove, IL: InterVarsity Press, © 1967). Used by permission of the publisher.*

Learning Objectives

Complete this book, and you'll know how to:

1) Define the basics of time management, and determine how you presently use time.

2) Apply time management techniques.

3) Identify and address both environmental and self-generated time-wasters.

4) Make the most of travel time.

5) Apply time management principles and techniques.

Workplace and Management Competencies mapping

For over 30 years, business and industry has utilized competency models to select employees. The trend to use competency-based approaches in education and training, assessment, and development of workers has experienced a more recent emergence within the Employment and Training Administration (ETA), a division of the United States Department of Labor.

The ETA's General Competency Model Framework spans a wide array of competencies from the more basic competencies, such as reading and writing, to more advanced occupation-specific competencies. The 50-Minute Manager Series finds its home in what the ETA refers to as the Workplace Competencies and the Management Competencies.

Time Management covers information vital to mastering the following competencies:

Workplace Competencies:

▶ Adaptability & Flexibility

▶ Planning & Organizing

Management Competencies:

▶ Monitoring Work

For a comprehensive mapping of 50-Minute Manager Series titles to the Workplace and Management competencies, visit *50minutemanager.com*

About the 50-Minute Manager Series

The 50-Minute Manager Series is designed to cover critical business and professional development topics in the shortest possible time. Our easy-to-read, easy-to-understand format can be used for self-study or for classroom training. With a wealth of hands-on exercises, the 50-Minute books keep you engaged and help you retain critical skills.

What You Need to Know

We designed the 50-Minute Manager Series to be as self-explanatory as possible. But there are a few things you should know before you begin the book.

Exercises

Exercises look like this:

EXERCISE TITLE

Questions and other information would be here.

Keep a pencil handy. Any time you see an exercise, you should try to complete it. If the exercise has specific answers, an answer key is provided in the appendix. (Some exercises ask you to think about your own opinions or situation; these types of exercises don't have answer keys.)

Forms

A heading like this means that the rest of the page is a form:

FORMHEAD

Forms are meant to be reusable. You might want to make a photocopy of a form before you fill it out, so that you can use it again later.

A Note to Instructors

We've tried to make the 50-Minute Manager Series books as useful as possible as classroom training manuals. Here are some of the features we provide for instructors:

▶ PowerPoint presentations

▶ Answer keys

▶ Assessments

▶ Customization

PowerPoint Presentations

You can download a PowerPoint presentation for this book from our Web site at *50minutemanager.com*

Answer keys

If an exercise has specific answers, an answer key will be provided in the appendix. (Some exercises ask you to think about your own opinions or situation; these types of exercises will not have answer keys.)

Assessments

For each 50-Minute Series book, we have developed a 35- to 50-item assessment. The assessment for this book is available at 50minutemanager.com. *Assessments should not be used in any employee-selection process.*

Customization

These books can be quickly and easily customized to meet your needs—from adding your logo to developing proprietary content. 50-Minute Manager books are available in print and electronic form. For more information on customization, see 50minutemanager.com.

PART 1

Time Management

Principles

"The best way to begin, is to begin."

—Marie Edmond Jones

In this part:

- ▶ The Basics of Time Management
- ▶ What Controls Your Time?
- ▶ Three Tests of Time
- ▶ Benefits of Better Time Utilization
- ▶ Prime Time
- ▶ Setting Priorities
- ▶ Criteria for Setting Priorities
- ▶ How to Control Your Use of Time
- ▶ Tips for Effective Time Management

The Basics of Time Management

Time is a unique resource. Day to day, everyone has the same amount. It can't be accumulated. You can't turn it on or off. It can't be replaced. It has to be spent at the rate of sixty seconds every minute.

Time management—like the management of other resources—benefits from analysis and planning. To understand and apply time management principles, you must know not only how you use time, but also what problems you encounter in using it wisely and what causes them. From this knowledge, you can improve your effectiveness and efficiency through better time management.

Time management is a personal process that must fit your style and circumstances. It takes a strong commitment to change old habits, but the principles in this book can lead to better time investment.

The questionnaire on the following page will assist you in looking at your current time management attitudes and practices. It will help identify things to concentrate on as you complete this book. When you've worked through this book, including the exercises and questionnaires, you will:

▶ Learn the three tests for using time wisely.

▶ Understand the importance of priorities and how to set them.

▶ Learn how to overcome the most common time-wasters.

▶ Learn to schedule work to take advantage of your most productive time.

▶ Learn how to make the best use of time when you travel.

▶ Learn how to analyze your use of time and plan for improvement

WE ALL GET 168 HOURS PER WEEK, HOW DO YOU USE YOURS?

Place a check (✓) in the column that best describes how you feel or act – U (Usually), S (Sometimes), or R (Rarely). Then review your responses and look for ways to improve your use of time.[1]

	U	S	R
1. Do you normally spend time the way you really want to?	❏	❏	❏
2. Do you often feel harried and obligated to do things you really don't want to do?	❏	❏	❏
3. Do you feel a sense of accomplishment from your work?	❏	❏	❏
4. Do you regularly work longer hours than your colleagues?	❏	❏	❏
5. Do you regularly take work home on evenings or weekends?	❏	❏	❏
6. Do you feel stress because of too much work?	❏	❏	❏
7. Do you feel guilty about your performance at work?	❏	❏	❏
8. Do you consider your job to be fun?	❏	❏	❏
9. Can you find blocks of uninterrupted time when you need to?	❏	❏	❏
10. Do you feel in control of your time?	❏	❏	❏
11. Do you exercise regularly?	❏	❏	❏
12. Do you take vacations or long weekends as often as you'd like?	❏	❏	❏
13. Do you put off doing the difficult, boring, or unpleasant parts of your job?	❏	❏	❏
14. Do you feel you must always be busy doing something productive?	❏	❏	❏
15. Do you feel guilty when you occasionally goof off?	❏	❏	❏

---

[1] Adapted from Successful Time Management by Jack D. Ferner, pp. 6-7 (NY: John Wiley & Sons, 1980). Used by permission of the publisher.

What Controls Your Time?

The best way to begin improving time management is to examine how you control your time. No one has total control over a daily schedule. Someone or something always makes demands. However, we all have some control—and probably more than we realize.

A portion of each day is structured by your working hours or school hours. But even within this structure, there are opportunities to select which tasks or activities to handle and what priority to assign to each of them. These discretionary choices allow you to control your time.

CONTROL OF YOUR TIME

Time at work should be used to pursue company objectives. In school, time should be spent in class or studying. Time is often controlled by specific tasks or assignments. However, some degree of freedom usually exists in any specific time period. How much control do you have over time at work or in school? (Circle one of the numbers below.)

Most Control	10	9	8	7	6	5	4	3	2	1	Least Control

Areas Where I Have Most Control   **Areas Where I Have Least Control**

_____   _____

_____   _____

_____   _____

_____   _____

_____   _____

_____   _____

_____   _____

_____   _____

Three Tests of Time

You must have specific, reliable information to determine where opportunities for improvement exist. The best way to analyze your current use of time is to keep a daily time log.

After this information has been recorded, examine it from three points of view: Necessity, Appropriateness, and Efficiency. This examination should allow you to identify tasks to eliminate or delegate and to find ways to increase efficiency through technology, new procedures, or personal work habits.

A careful analysis can often earn you another eight to 10 hours each week to spend on activities of your choice.

1 **The Test of Necessity:** Scrutinize each activity to be sure it's necessary—not just nice, but necessary. Look for activities that have outlived their usefulness (e.g., monthly reports that generate information that's no longer used.) This test of necessity should help confine tasks to those that are essential.

2 **The Test of Appropriateness:** Once essential tasks are identified, determine who should perform them (i.e., appropriateness in terms of department or skill level.) There are probably activities that could be given to others. You may find you're doing work below your skill level that can easily be reassigned.

3 **The Test of Efficiency:** Examine the tasks that remain. Once you're satisfied that the work you're doing is necessary, ask yourself, "Is there a better way?" For example, you might use better technology or better procedures to handle recurring activities.

Note: This book uses examples drawn from the business world, but the same principles might apply to activities at school, at home, or in community service.

ANALYZE FOR EFFECTIVE TIME UTILIZATION

Using the three tests, list some opportunities for more effective use of your time.

The Test of Necessity:

_____

_____

_____

_____

The Test of Appropriateness:

_____

_____

_____

_____

The Test of Efficiency:

_____

_____

_____

_____

There Are Only Three Ways to Make Better Use of Your Time

1. Discontinue low-priority tasks or activities.
2. Be more efficient at what you do.
3. Find someone else to take some of your work.

Benefits of Better Time Utilization

When you make better use of time, you can benefit from activities such as:

▶ **Career Planning**: Set a course for your future and lay out a plan to achieve it. Be proactive and take charge of your own destiny.

▶ **Reading**: Staying current is increasingly important in today's complex world. More time will allow you to read job-related materials, study new subjects, or learn more about a leisure activity.

▶ **Communicating**: Extra time will allow you to initiate and improve both work and personal relationships.

▶ **Relaxing**: You need to plan time for relaxation. When you don't take time off from the daily grind, your health may suffer or you may burn out.

▶ **Thinking**: Improved methods and opportunities are a result of innovation. More time will allow you to develop strategies and think through plans to establish and achieve new challenges.

THINK ABOUT IT

What's getting squeezed out of your day by other demands on your time? How would it benefit you to devote more time to these activities?

_____

_____

_____

_____

_____

_____

_____

_____

CASE STUDY: The New Supervisor

Three months ago, Sheila looked forward to her promotion to supervisor. After four years in the department, she was confident of her abilities and knew her staff was capable and experienced.

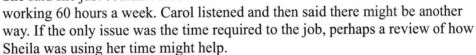

Today, Sheila isn't so sure she was cut out to be a supervisor. There seems to be no end to her workday. During office hours, her day is filled assigning work and reviewing results. Also, there's a steady flow of visitors, and the phone rings constantly. In the evening, when she'd like to relax, she has to take care of administrative matters, such as reading mail, answering letters, preparing budgets, and completing performance appraisals.

In frustration, Sheila asked her friend Carol to join her for lunch. She told Carol she was thinking about giving up her supervisor's job. She said she just couldn't face a lifetime of working 60 hours a week. Carol listened and then said there might be another way. If the only issue was the time required to the job, perhaps a review of how Sheila was using her time might help.

After listening to Sheila describe a typical week, Carol asked the following questions:

▶ Since she described her staff as capable and experienced, why was Sheila spending so much time assigning work and reviewing results?

▶ Who were the drop-in visitors? Could some be screened out?

▶ Could the department secretary take phone calls and refer some to others or have non-urgent calls returned at a more convenient time?

▶ Could some of Sheila's work be done by someone else?

With this in mind, Sheila decided to take a closer look at her use of time.

CONTINUED

Consider Sheila's situation and answer the following questions.

1. Is she delegating? ☐ Yes ☐ No

2. If her visitors are employees, how might she avoid interruptions?

   _____

   _____

   _____

3. Should Sheila consider establishing a "quiet time" when she'd receive no calls or visitors? If so, when might be the best time of day?

   _____

   _____

   _____

4. Sheila feels she should assign all departmental work and review all results. Is there a more efficient way?

   _____

   _____

   _____

5. In what other ways could Sheila gain more control over her use of time?

   _____

   _____

   _____

HOW WOULD YOU HANDLE THESE SITUATIONS?

Listed below are situations where an opportunity exists to improve the use of time. Read each example and then check (✓) the choice you feel is the best response.

1. As Jean reviews time cards each week, she spends two hours summarizing the hours of employees who have exceptions, such as sick leave or vacation time. She's aware that the payroll department gathers this same information and provides it to all department heads. What should she do?

    a. Continue summarizing the information.

    b. Stop summarizing the information.

    c. Point out the duplication to her own supervisor and request permission to stop doing the work.

2. Rachel likes interviewing candidates. She's excellent at matching candidates with job openings. Now that she's manager, she still spends about five hours a week interviewing, even though she has a staff to handle this work. As a result, she often takes work home. What should Rachel do?

    a. Stay with her present practice. She's the supervisor and has the right to act as she sees fit.

    b. Delegate some of the administrative work to her staff so that she can keep interviewing.

    c. Stop interviewing except when the workload exceeds staff capacity.

    d. Have her staff interview some applicants to narrow the field to the one or two best candidates.

3. Carlos distributes a computer-generated report to field offices quarterly. A couple of his field colleagues told him that they don't use the report. What should he do?

    a. Ignore the comments and continue to distribute the report.

    b. Stop distributing the report and see what happens.

    c. Survey all field offices and recommend a change in the report based on what's found.

4. When Alexis assumed her present job, she noticed the quality of expense summaries she received from accounting was inadequate. Expenses were incorrectly allocated, and often two months passed before accounts were correct. In order to have timely, accurate information, she now spends six hours a week keeping her own records. What should she do?

   a. Continue keeping her own records. It's the only way to know they're done correctly.

   b. Stop keeping her own records and use those furnished by the accounting department.

   c. Meet with the accounting departement to work out a way to get the information she needs.

5. Patrick is an assistant in the personnel department. Several times each month, employees ask him to work up an estimate of their retirement benefits. He does them by hand, and each estimate takes 45 minutes. What should Patrick do?

   a. Continue the practice; it seems to work okay.

   b. Refuse to prepare estimates except for employees planning to retire within a year.

   c. Develop a computer-generated summary sheet that can be personalized.

6. Janice receives 25 to 40 inquiries daily from members about the association's medical insurance coverage. Each requires a personal reply. This part of her job consumes most of her time, leaving little time for her other duties. What should she do?

   a. Continue providing this service to members—they're entitled to it.

   b. Develop a form letter and mail it with a plan summary in response to all inquiries.

   c. Study recent inquiries to find which questions are asked most. Publish a list of frequently asked questions to cut down on the number of direct inquiries.

The author feels that "c" is the best response to each question.

Prime Time

Keep your energy cycle in mind when considering a daily schedule. Some people are at their best early in the morning. Others peak in the afternoon. Your peak is called your *prime time*. Whenever possible, plan your daily schedule to take advantage of your prime time. Try to schedule work that requires concentration, creativity, and thought during your prime time. Leave more mechanical tasks until after lunch, if your prime time is in the morning.

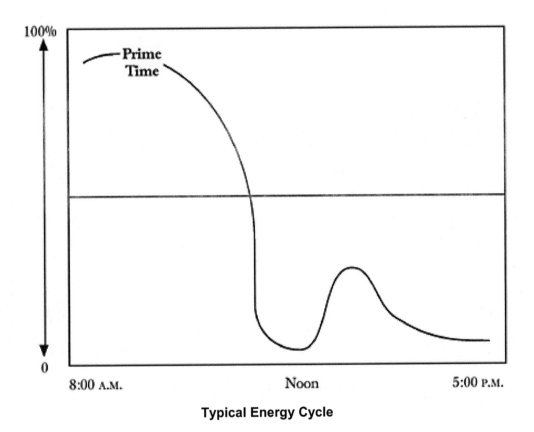

Typical Energy Cycle

On the following page is an exercise to help you visualize your energy cycle.

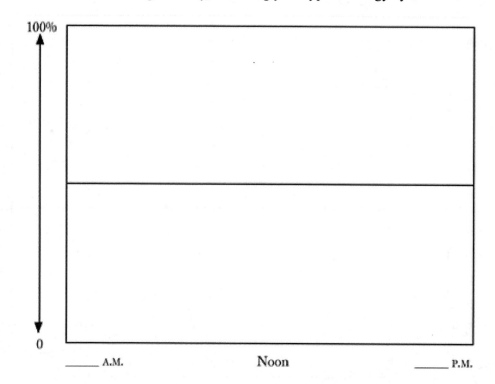

CHART YOUR ENERGY CYCLE

Fill in the beginning and ending time of your day on the following diagram. Then draw a line through the day, reflecting your typical energy cycle.

100%

0

_____ A.M.   Noon   _____ P.M.

1. Do you arrange your workday or class load to take advantage of your prime time?   ☐ Yes   ☐ No

2. What could you do differently to better utilize your period of peak energy?

_____

_____

_____

_____

Setting Priorities

When opportunities exceed resources, decisions must be made. Nowhere is this more apparent than in the use of time. Since time can't be manufactured, you must decide what to do and what not to do.

Setting priorities in the use of time is a two-step process:

1. List things that need to be done.

2. Prioritize items on the list.

The ABC Method

Use the *ABC Method* to determine your priorities by assigning each item on your list to one of the following priorities:

A. "Must Do"—these are the critical items. Items with this priority might include management directives, customer requirements, deadlines, or opportunities for success or advancement.

B. "Should Do"—these are items of medium value. Items with this priority may contribute to improved performance but aren't essential or don't have critical deadlines.

C. "Nice to Do"—this is the lowest-value category. While interesting or fun, these items could be eliminated, postponed, or scheduled for slack periods.

Priorities change over time. As an important deadline approaches, today's B may become tomorrow's A . Likewise, today's A may become tomorrow's C, if it doesn't get accomplished in time or as circumstances change.

Don't spend significant time on a low-priority task. Instead, try to focus first on high-priority tasks. Use the form on next page to practice setting priorities.

Criteria for Setting Priorities

▶ **Judgment**. You're the best judge of what you have to do.

▶ **Evaluation**. As you compare tasks or activities, it should become clear that some are higher priority than others. You should always be guided by the question, "What's the best use of my time right now?"

▶ **Timing**. Deadlines have a way of dictating priorities. Setting a good start time is critical to finishing a project by its deadline.

THINK ABOUT IT

List your priorities for the week. Label each one A, B, or C.

_____

_____

_____

_____

_____

_____

What problems have you encountered in prioritizing demands on your time?

_____

_____

_____

_____

_____

_____

SELF-ASSESSMENT QUESTIONNAIRE

The following statements summarize the principles presented in Part 1 of this book. Check those that apply to you. Review items you didn't check to see if they represent an opportunity for future efficiency.

▶ I know when my prime time occurs.

▶ I adjusted my daily routine to make the best use of my prime time.

▶ I wrote a summary of my responsibilities.

▶ I listed my objectives for the next quarter.

▶ I prioritized my tasks.

▶ I eliminated unnecessary and inappropriate tasks.

▶ I studied ways to improve efficiency in handling routine matters.

▶ I delegate whenever possible.

▶ I prepare a daily "things to do" list.

▶ I leave some time for the unexpected each day.

▶ I realize that I can't do everything and must choose the best alternatives.

THINK ABOUT IT

Which time management principles will be of greatest benefit to you? How do you plan to use these principles?

_____

_____

_____

_____

REVIEW WORKSHEET

1. Following are ways I can make better use of my time:

    _____

    _____

    _____

    _____

2. The major roadblocks to a more effective and efficient use of my time are:

    _____

    _____

    _____

    _____

3. If I "found" five hours a week, here's how I would use that time:

    _____

    _____

    _____

    _____

"I start my day by making a list of everything I need to do…
and who I can get to do it for me."

How to Control Your Use of Time

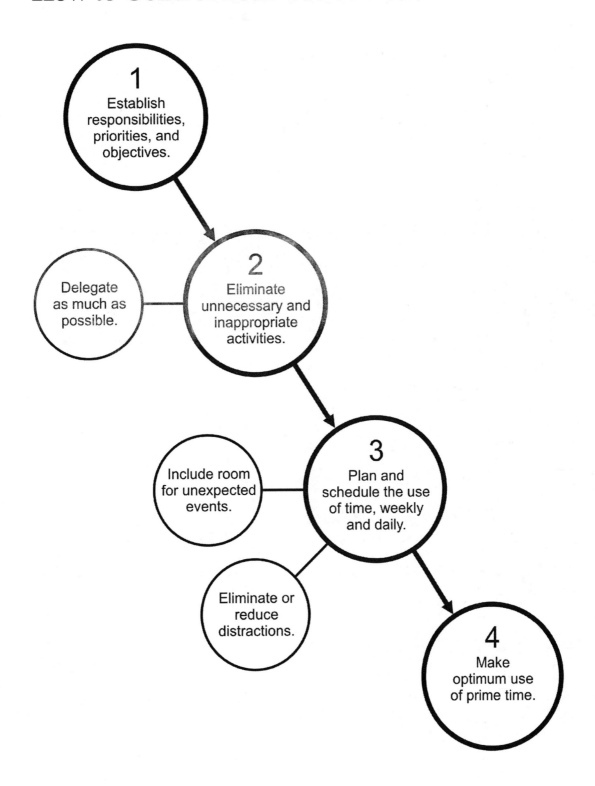

1 Establish responsibilities, priorities, and objectives.

2 Eliminate unnecessary and inappropriate activities.

Delegate as much as possible.

3 Plan and schedule the use of time, weekly and daily.

Include room for unexpected events.

Eliminate or reduce distractions.

4 Make optimum use of prime time.

Tips for Effective Time Management

1 List and prioritize weekly objectives.

2 Make a daily to-do list and prioritize it.

3 Devote primary attention to your A's.

4 Handle each piece of paper only once.

5 Continually ask, "What's the best use of my time right now?"

> *Time is the coin of your life. It is the only coin you have, and only you can determine how it will be spent. Be careful lest you let other people spend it for you."*

–Carl Sandberg

Part Summary

In this part, you learned how to define the **basics of time management**. You learned how to understand **what controls your time** now, and you learned the benefits of **better time utilization**. You learned how to find your personal **prime time** and how to **set priorities** and **control your use of time**.

Time Management Techniques

> *He who every morning plans the transaction of the day and follows out that plan, carries a thread that will guide him through the maze of the most busy life. But where no plan is laid, where the disposal of time is surrendered merely to the chance of incidence, chaos will soon reign."*
>
> –Victor Hugo

In this part:

▶ Planning

▶ Long-Term Planning Aids

▶ Short-Term Planning Aids

▶ Characteristics of Good Planners

Planning

Planning is a complex process. Some people are good at it; others aren't. Some seem so caught up in activities and deadlines that they claim there's no time to plan. Yet planning is the key to relieving the stress of too little time. It's the way to structure your future.

Planning makes two contributions that bring order to your life. First, it tells you how to get from where you are to where you want to be. Second, it identifies the resources required to get you there. Planning allows you to work on and complete a project on schedule.

Planning can be long-term or short-term. In this book, long-term plans describe what you expect to accomplish during the next three months or any project that takes more than a week. Short-term plans cover what you expect to accomplish in a day or a week, including steps toward longer-term objectives.

MY TIME FRAME

Long-Term Objectives. These are my objectives for the next quarter, along with any projects that will take longer than a week:

_____

_____

_____

_____

Short-Term Goals. These are the things that need doing this week including steps toward longer-term objectives:

_____

_____

_____

_____

Long-Term Planning Aids

Planning aids are a critical part of effective time management. It simply isn't possible to remember everything. These common planning aids are described on the following pages:

▶ Action-Planning Worksheet

▶ Milestone Chart

▶ PERT Diagram

From these alternatives, you can select the technique that best fits the type of work you do. Using a planning aid will help bring order to your life.

A note of caution—don't get too elaborate. Don't spend more time on planning aids than is necessary. In other words, planning should save you time, not *cost* you time.

Regardless of the technique you choose, you should record all activities on a calendar. Note the due dates for each action step as well as project completion dates. When others are responsible for a step in your plan, ensure you have a follow-up date assigned. Also, always know who has responsibility for each step and the date the action is to be completed.

THINK ABOUT IT

What opportunities are there for which you can use long-term planning aids in your area of responsibility?

_____

_____

_____

_____

_____

_____

Action-Planning Worksheet

Action-Planning worksheets can vary greatly in complexity. The simplest show only the steps required to complete a project. Additional information can be beginning dates, targeted completion dates, cost estimates, and those responsible for each task.

A sample Action-Planning worksheet is shown below; a blank one for your use follows.

Example

Action-Planning Worksheet

Objective: *Publish a Work-Planning and Review workbook by May 31.*

Action Step	Est. Time	Target Date	Assigned Responsibility
1. Write draft	15 days	Apr. 15	Self
2. Type draft	10 days	Apr. 25	Secretary
3. Proofread	5 days	Apr. 20	Self & secretary
4. Draw cover	5 days	Apr. 30	Graphics
5. Type final	10 days	May 10	Key entry
6. Proofread	3 days	May 13	Self & secretary
7. Make corrections	2 days	May 15	Key entry
8. Draw figures	5 days	May 15	Graphics
9. Reproduce	15 days	May 30	Print shop
10. Deliver books		May 31	Print shop

Action-Planning Worksheet

Objective:

Action Step	Target Date	Cost		Assigned Responsibility
		Dollars	Time	

Milestone Chart

A milestone chart graphically displays the relationship of project steps. To create a milestone chart, begin by listing the steps required to finish the project; then estimate the time required for each step. Record the steps on the left side of the chart, with dates shown along the bottom. Draw a line across the chart for each step, starting at the planned beginning date and ending on the projected completion date of that step. Once completed, you should be able to see the flow of the action steps and their sequence (including steps that can be underway at the same time).

The milestone chart's usefulness can be improved by also charting actual progress. This is usually done by drawing a line in a different color under the original line to show actual beginning and actual completion dates of each step.

Example

Objective: *Publish a Work-Planning and Review workbook by May 31.*

Action Steps with Time Estimates:

1. Write draft	15 days	6. Proofread	3 days
2. Type draft	10 days	7. Make corrections	2 days
3. Proofread	5 days	8. Draw figures	5 days
4. Draw cover	5 days	9. Reproduce	15 days
5. Type final	10 days	10. Deliver books	

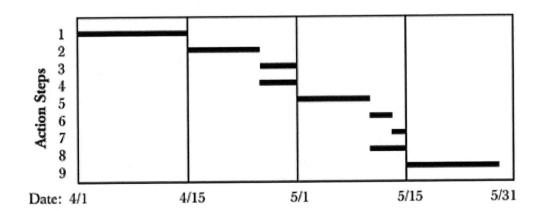

DRAW A MILESTONE CHART

Select a project and practice drawing a Milestone Chart.

Objective: _____

_____

Action Steps with Time Estimates:

_____ _____ | _____ _____

_____ _____ | _____ _____

_____ _____ | _____ _____

_____ _____ | _____ _____

_____ _____ | _____ _____

_____ _____ | _____ _____

_____ _____ | _____ _____

_____ _____ | _____ _____

PERT Diagram

A PERT diagram represents an added degree of sophistication in the planning process. PERT stands for:

Program

Evaluation &

Review

Technique

To draw a PERT diagram, list the project steps and estimate the time required to complete each step. Then draw a network of relationships among the steps. The number of the step is shown in a circle, and the time to complete the step is shown on the line leading to the next circle. Steps that must be completed in order are shown on one path to clarify proper sequencing. Steps that can be underway at the same time are shown on different paths.

A PERT diagram not only shows the relationship among various steps in a project but also serves as an easy way to calculate the critical path. The critical path is the longest time path through the network and identifies essential steps that must be completed on time to avoid delaying the completion of the total project. The critical path is shown as a broken line in the example on the next page.

You can increase the usefulness of a PERT diagram by coloring each step as it's completed. The actual duration may be written over the estimated duration to maintain a running tally of actual versus planned time along the critical path.

Example

Objective: *Publish a Work-Planning and Review workbook by May 31.*

Action Steps with Time Estimates:

1. Write draft	15 days	6. Proofread	3 days
2. Type draft	10 days	7. Make corrections	2 days
3. Proofread	5 days	8. Draw figures	5 days
4. Draw cover	5 days	9. Reproduce	15 days
5. Type final	10 days	10. Deliver books	

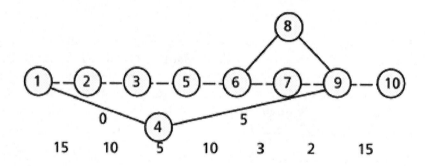

"There aren't enough hours in the day, Rogers. See to it."

PRACTICE DRAWING A PERT DIAGRAM

Objective: _____

_____

_____

Action Steps with Time Estimates:

PERT Diagram:

Short-Term Planning Aids

Action steps in long-term plans must be integrated and prioritized with your other demands. These discrete steps become part of your short-term plans. Short-term plans are best developed and scheduled on both a weekly and a daily basis.

Weekly Plans

A weekly plan should describe what you want to accomplish by the end of the week and the activities required to get you there. Plans for the following week can be developed on Friday, over the weekend, or on Monday morning. (Many people use commuting time for this activity.)

Weekly worksheets may be simple or complex. The following example can serve as a starting point for your short-term plans.

Once completed, your worksheet should be kept handy for frequent reference. Daily activities should be prioritized and transferred to a daily calendar.

Example

Things to Do This Week

Read Chapters 5 and 6 for World History class.

Outline term paper for American Government class.

Complete project for English Composition class.

Work three hours at American Red Cross.

Wash car.

Clean room.

Line up date for spring dance.

Weekly Planning Worksheet

For the week of: _____

Objectives:

1. _____
2. _____
3. _____

Activities	A/B/C Priority	Est. Time	Assigned Day

This sheet may be copied for your use.

Daily Plans

The planning process is the best use of your time each day. If you make a habit of using a daily calendar, many of your activities will already be recorded. This is the best place to start your list of "things to do today."

A daily, prioritized list focuses attention on your most important objectives. Work from high- to low-priority items. If unexpected demands come up, assess their priority and handle them accordingly. Don't let something unexpected distract you. At the end of each day, review what was accomplished and carry forward any items that need completing. Reprioritize these with tomorrow's new items.

The format for your list isn't important. It can be written anywhere—on a calendar, a plain sheet of paper, a form that you develop, or as a document on your computer. Many stationery stores have a variety of planning forms available.

Use your to-do list to lay out a daily schedule. It should reflect meetings and appointments, plus time to accomplish other priority items on your list.

The example below illustrates how simple a daily form can be. The example on the next page is more elaborate.

Example

Things to Do Today

Make travel arrangements.

Attend budget review @ 10:00 a.m.

Complete salary proposals.

Reserve conference room for Wed.

Call insurance agent.

Make dentist appointment.

Daily Planning Worksheet

Date: _____

Tasks to Complete	Done	Appointments to Keep
		7:00
		8:00
		9:00
		10:00
		11:00
		12:00
Phone Calls to Make	**Done**	
		1:00
		2:00
		3:00
People to See	**Done**	4:00
		5:00
		6:00
		7:00

Characteristics of Good Planners

The following statements describe how people view various aspects of planning. Which of these do you think reflect good planning?

▶ Identify two time horizons and operate within them. Anticipating events allows things that contribute to achieving long-term objectives to get done in the near term.

▶ An up-to-date calendar can be a helpful planning tool. However, detailed project plans must be developed before valid entries can be made on a master calendar.

▶ When things begin to get hectic, a "things to do today" list helps focus attention on the highest priority items.

▶ Action-Planning worksheets, milestone charts, and PERT diagrams can be excellent planning aids.

▶ Plan contact with colleagues and staff to help minimize the disruption of their schedules. One way to do this is to use a conference planner.

▶ The most effective approaches to planning are those tailored to meet individual needs. Concepts, procedures, and worksheets are all subject to modification to fit individual circumstances.

THINK ABOUT IT

Using the checklist as a guide, how can you improve your use of time?

_____

_____

_____

_____

_____

_____

Part Summary

In this part, you learned the importance of setting **long-term objectives** and **short-term goals**. You learned how to use long-term planning aids, including **action-planning worksheets**, **milestone charts**, and **PERT diagrams**. You learned how to use short-term planning aids, including **daily** and **weekly plans**. Finally, you learned the **characteristics of good planners**.

Avoiding

Wasted Time

> "It has been my observation that most people get ahead during the time that others waste time."
>
> –Henry Ford

In this part:

▶ Common Time-Wasters

▶ Self-Generated Time-Wasters

▶ Environmental Time-Wasters

▶ When Things Go Wrong

Common Time-Wasters

Everyone wastes time. It's part of being human. Some wasted time can be constructive, because it helps you relax or otherwise reduces tension. Other wasted time, however, can be frustrating. This is especially true when time is wasted because you're doing something that keeps you from attending to priorities.

The key question is, what else might you be doing that's of a higher priority? Taking a break, communicating with associates, talking on the phone, and reading aren't time-wasters unless they keep you from higher priority activities.

Time-wasters usually originate from two sources. One is your environment, and the other is yourself. Some typical examples of each are listed in the table that follows. The next few pages concentrate on ways for you to recognize and manage your most frequent time-wasters.

Examples of Common Time-Wasters

Self-Generated	Environmental
Disorganization	Phone calls, mail, email
Procrastination	Surfing the Internet
Socializing	Visitors
Acceptance	Waiting for someone
Perfectionism	Unproductive meetings
Risk Avoidance	Crises

Self-Generated Time-Wasters

Self-generated time-wasters are a result of your unique work habits and personal characteristics. By spending time understanding your personal time-wasters, you can begin to overcome the most significant ones.

Disorganization

If you spend time searching for misplaced items, or waste time due to distractions which cause you to start and stop several times before a task is completed, then you need to evaluate your work area.

Disorganization is a key culprit in wasted time. Disorganization shows up in the layout of a work area—whether it's a desk or a computer desktop. Check out your layout. Is it efficient? Is it organized to minimize effort? Is there a free flow of materials and movement? Have you considered the placement of equipment, such as telephone and computer, the proximity of supplies that are frequently used, and your accessibility to active files?

Next, focus on your desk. Is it cluttered? How much time do you waste looking for things you know are there but can't find? When was the last time you used some of the items in and on your desk? Perhaps a housecleaning is in order.

"A few messages came in while you were at lunch."

The old axiom, "A place for everything and everything in its place," is good advice for organizing information you need. Files for work in progress should be set up and kept handy. Everything relating to a project should be kept in one file folder. Files should be indexed for quick reference. Call-up procedures are required for items that need future action. A folder for current items received by mail, telephone, or visit should be maintained and checked daily to see what needs to be done.

Finally, organize your approach to work. Once begun, tasks should be completed. If interrupted, don't immediately jump to a new task. Assess the priority of a request and avoid getting involved in any new activity until it becomes your top priority. If an interruption comes by phone or personal visit, simply return to the task you were working on as soon as the interruption ends.

THINK ABOUT IT

How can you change your work area to improve efficiency?

_____

_____

_____

A Personal Filing System

It isn't necessary to be too logical. It's your system, and no one else will be using it, so it needs to make sense only to you.

Use a limited number of categories when organizing a desk or a computer. For example, you may find the following five to be adequate:

1 **Projects.** In this category are individual files with information related to various projects you're working on.

2 **Instant Tasks.** This category should include folders on little jobs to fill in your time when you have a few minutes—perhaps low-priority letters to be answered or general-interest articles.

3 **Self-Development.** This category contains folders related to training: books, articles, etc.

4 **Ideas.** This category contains items you wish to investigate further to improve your operation.

5 **Background Information.** This category is a resource for various things with which you're involved. Keep separate folders by topic and refer to them when you need statistics, examples, quotations, etc.

It may be a good idea to color-code by priority within each category to draw attention to important items. This is easily accomplished by using highlighters of various colors and marking individual folders.

Keep your filing current, so that time won't be wasted searching for an item.

Clean your files periodically to keep the volume of material to an essential minimum. Doing so also reduces time going through files when you're looking for something.

Procrastination

We all put things off. Typically, these items include boring, difficult, unpleasant, or onerous tasks that ultimately need completing. When this happens to you, consider the following:

▶ Set a deadline to complete the task and stick with it.

▶ Build in a reward system. For example, tell yourself, "When I finish that task, I'm going to enjoy a nice meal with my significant other." Or, "I won't go home until I finish this task."

▶ Arrange with someone (an associate or colleague) to follow up with you routinely about progress on tasks you tend to put off.

▶ Do undesirable tasks early in the day so that you can be done with them.

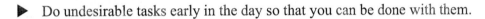

TIPS FOR DEALING WITH PROCRASTINATION

Check the ideas you think would be helpful.

1. Set a deadline. ❑

2. Do the unpleasant task first. ❑

3. Set up a reward system. ❑

4. Break the job into small pieces. ❑

5. Arrange for follow-up. ❑

6. Do it now! ❑

Personal Needs

Many self-generated time-wasters are the result of efforts to satisfy personal needs such as social acceptance, perfection, and risk avoidance. Most people are unaware of this process. For example, it's most uncommon to hear someone say, "I have a high need for acceptance and therefore will do whatever you ask in order to satisfy that need." Rather, an individual takes on extra work, responds to every request, and feels good when others express appreciation. In the meantime, other, more important work may be left undone. To take a cursory look at your needs profile, complete the Personal Needs Assessment Questionnaire on the following pages.

THINK ABOUT IT

What's your reaction to the idea that your personal needs may take you away from higher priority work? List some examples where this may have happened.

_____

_____

_____

_____

_____

_____

_____

_____

_____

_____

_____

_____

_____

PERSONAL NEEDS ASSESSMENT

Indicate the extent to which you agree or disagree with each statement by entering one of these values.

> 5 = Completely agree   4 = Tend to agree   3 = Uncertain
> 2 = Tend to disagree   1 = Completely disagree

_____ 1. I couldn't work in a job that required me to work alone most or all of the time.

_____ 2. What others think of me is extremely important to me.

_____ 3. I worry about mistakes I've made in my work.

_____ 4. I'm terribly embarrassed by errors in my work.

_____ 5. I prefer to be a member of a team rather than work alone.

_____ 6. I'm pleased when others ask for assistance and will do everything I can to comply.

_____ 7. I'm not satisfied until I've done my very best on any given task.

_____ 8. I spend a lot of time analyzing possibilities before acting.

_____ 9. A friendly social atmosphere is an important part of a good place to work.

_____ 10. I frequently subordinate my views and desires to those of others.

_____ 11. To be sure something is done correctly, I do it myself.

_____ 12. Rules and regulations are to be understood and strictly followed.

_____ 13. It's necessary and appropriate to take a portion of a workday for friendly conversation.

_____ 14. I find it difficult to end conversations, even when they interfere with my work.

CONTINUED

5 = Completely agree   4 = Tend to agree   3 = Uncertain
2 = Tend to disagree   1 = Completely disagree

_____ 15. I spend a lot of time correcting or redoing work done by others.

_____ 16. I prefer a lot of organization and structure in my job.

_____ 17. I take a great deal of pride in the number of friends I have.

_____ 18. I often guess at what someone wants rather than be embarrassed by asking for more information.

_____ 19. People who turn out less-than-perfect quality work are either careless or lazy.

_____ 20. I have a need to include the thoughts and wishes of others in decisions I make that might affect them.

Scoring

List your responses on the lines below that correspond to each statement. Add the values of your responses and record the total for each column.

Social Interaction	Acceptance	Perfection	Risk Avoidance
1. _____	2. _____	3. _____	4. _____
5. _____	3. _____	7. _____	8. _____
9. _____	10. _____	11. _____	12. _____
13. _____	14. _____	15. _____	16. _____
17. _____	18. _____	19. _____	20. _____

Totals:

_____   _____   _____   _____

A score of 16 or more indicates a high need. A score of 20 or more indicates a need sufficiently strong to be a potential problem in your effective use of time.

Needs Profile Analysis

Social Interaction

Many jobs provide adequate opportunity to satisfy social needs; others do not. Problems can arise when people with high social needs occupy jobs with little built-in opportunity to satisfy those needs. When this occurs, needs are typically satisfied in nonproductive ways.

People with unsatisfied high social needs tend to waste not only their time but also the time of others in close proximity. They tend to be drop-in visitors with no particular agenda—or a very superficial one. Having dropped in, their conversations often are difficult to terminate.

If you fall into this category, two ideas may help:

First, respect the time of others. Ask if he or she has time to talk or if it would be better for you to come back later. Observe your conversational partner. Does he or she seem anxious to do something else? Watch for such things as standing up and moving away, glancing at papers, or even returning to work by writing, typing at the keyboard, or making calculations.

Second, develop ways to have your social needs satisfied productively. Consider getting together with colleagues at lunch, scheduling breaks with others in advance, requesting assignments to ad hoc work teams, and getting involved in group activities after work.

Acceptance

Many work groups provide an adequate opportunity to satisfy high acceptance needs. The self-worth of individual group members is confirmed through normal interaction and feedback. This process is further enhanced when group members cooperate and support each other. They don't make unreasonable demands on one another, and they work together to minimize the impact of demands from outside the group.

People with unsatisfied high acceptance needs tend to take on too much work. They often are viewed as "easy," and others take advantage of them. Doing what others ask is the price paid for acceptance, confirmation of self-worth, and being liked. It's often a very high price in terms of alternate use of time. Time used responding to such requests may be wasted when it takes you away from higher-priority work.

If you score high in this category, the following ideas may help you gain better control over the use of your time:

First, look for ways to provide confirmation of worth. You can do this in two ways. As you address a task, determine the significance of the task and the contribution it can make to your organization. Then, give it your best effort. When you finish, reflect on and experience the pride of having completed the task and done it well. Be willing to pat yourself on the back figuratively. Don't depend solely on others for confirmation of your value.

Second, take inventory of the things you do well. Frequently, attention is focused on what isn't done well, i.e., where improvement is required. However, by doing this, a person's positive qualities are often taken for granted or ignored. An inventory of what you do well can counterbalance this tendency. When making your inventory, include both work and non-work items. Your goal is to create a long list, so include everything you can think of, and don't be too critical.

Finally, you must learn to deal with requests that come your way. Basically, you do this by learning to say "no" or at least "later." When someone asks you to do something, question its priority or importance. Don't let your own judgment be overshadowed by the organizational rank or intensity of the person making the request. Compare the priority of the request to the priority of what you'd otherwise be doing and use one of the following responses, as appropriate:

- ▶ "I can take care of that, but what I'm doing right now will be delayed. Is your request more important?

- ▶ "I'll be glad to handle that for you. However, I can't get to it until I finish what I'm doing. That will be…"

- ▶ "I'm sorry, but I don't have time to take on any new work. I'll call you when my schedule frees up."

- ▶ "I appreciate your vote of confidence but just can't work it into my schedule at this time. Sorry."

- ▶ "I'm sorry, I just can't do it. Have you considered asking…"

Perfection

Some tasks require very high quality output. As such, spending extra time checking and rechecking to ensure nearly-perfect performance is justified. However, many things don't require that level of quality. The key is to distinguish between those that require high quality and those that don't. Then, you can invest your time to achieve near-perfect results when required but won't waste time to attain perfection if it's unnecessary.

People who score low in this category (less than 10) may also waste time. Because of low quality standards, they may have to redo work that doesn't meet minimum standards of acceptability. Investing a little more time could result in substantial savings by eliminating the need to do something twice.

If this area is a problem for you, try the following techniques:

First, obtain a clear understanding of the quality level expected by the one assigning you the work. Ask questions like those below.

- ▶ Do you want a precise or an approximate answer?
- ▶ How much time and money can be spent to achieve a quality outcome?
- ▶ What quality level is expected?
- ▶ What's the cutoff on your range of acceptable quality?

Secondly, remember that time and effort invested in quality assurance shouldn't exceed the costs of potential error. You need a positive return on investment. To achieve this, you need to estimate the cost of potential error. If it's low, you can't afford to spend a lot of time to eliminate all the errors. If the cost is high, you obviously should take the time.

The potential costs of perfection can be great. When standards are too high, there will be very few times when they're met. This often leads to disappointment due to infrequent opportunities to experience success. Constant disappointment can have a severe negative impact on people's attitude.

Risk Avoidance

People with a high need to avoid risk typically take more time studying and analyzing options, checking with others to obtain concurrence, and waiting (or hesitating) to take action. Again, there may be times when any or all of these time-consuming activities are justified, but a problem arises when there's a lack of differentiation based on some valid criterion.

If risk avoidance is a problem for you, try the following techniques:

First, examine what's at stake when you find yourself taking more time than justified before rendering a decision or taking action. What's at risk? What will happen if it doesn't work out? Will you be embarrassed? Will you get fired? Will someone be seriously injured? Will the company lose a lot of money?

Then, explore the question: What will happen if it *does* work out? Will you get what you want? Will you meet the deadline? Will you save the company money? Will it improve the business?

Finally, compare the potential payoff and the potential cost of the opportunity you face. Which is more likely to occur? Is the potential payoff worth the risk? If so, move forward with conviction. If not, abandon the idea and don't look back.

There simply is no way to eliminate all risk. It's a normal part of life brought about by an inability to foresee the future. Foolish action, obviously, is to be avoided, but calculated risks should be taken when there's a high probability of a positive outcome.

THINK ABOUT IT

How do you see yourself as a risk-taker? Are there some responsibilities where you're more willing to take risks than others?

_____

_____

_____

_____

_____

_____

Environmental Time-Wasters

Even if you're well organized and making effective use of time, there will always be interruptions and distractions from outside sources. Here are ideas for handling some of the most common ones.

Phone Calls

For many, phone calls are a constant interruption. You can't eliminate all of them. You can, however, limit the amount of time they take. If you're fortunate enough to have someone answer your phone or to have a display phone with caller ID, then calls should be screened. Review which calls need a personal follow-up and delegate the others. Messages should be taken during periods when you don't wish to be interrupted.

When talking on the phone, limit social conversation. Provide short answers to questions. End the conversation, in a polite way, when it has achieved its business purpose.

Mail/Email

A third distraction is mail and email. If possible, have someone sort your mail into four separate piles: 1) action, 2) information only, 3) route to others, and 4) toss.

Handle each piece of mail only *once*. As you read it, decide what action is required and then take that action, even if it's putting it into an action file. "Information only" mail can be saved and read at a more convenient time (e.g., while commuting or waiting for appointments, over lunch, or in the evening). You can save time by responding to some mail by telephone or email. If information is requested, can someone else provide it by telephone or email?

Eliminate junk email. Consider using an email service that allows mail only from approved senders. Also, it's much more efficient to distinguish personal and business mail by using separate email accounts. Set up file folders in your email account. Keeping email files on your computer allows you read it off line. As soon as you've read or acted upon a message, delete it or file it in a specific folder. This eliminates rereading messages and unclutters your inbox.

Surfing the Internet

The Internet can be seductive. A news headline captures your attention, and you spend several minutes reading interesting but irrelevant information. It takes discipline and commitment to stay out of this trap.

If the option is available, customize your start page so you have your most-used links, news, and other information at your fingertips. Also, bookmark the websites you visit and save them in folders. Organize these folders by subject, and arrange them so the frequently used sites are at the top. Delete inactive or unused ones to unclutter your bookmark folders.

If you read a lot of material from websites, download the pages to your computer's hard drive and read them at your leisure. You can even save these pages to a flash drive and read them on your laptop while commuting or waiting for appointments. This saves you from having to absorb online material immediately and is also an effective use of your time.

Visitors

Controlling time taken up by visitors requires both courtesy and judgment. As a starting point, limit the number of people you invite to your work area. If you need to meet with a colleague at your facility, go to his or her work area. This way you can simply excuse yourself when your task is accomplished. It's often more difficult to get people to leave your area than it is for you to leave theirs.

Discourage drop-in visitors by turning your desk away from the door. When people see you're busy, they tend to not interrupt. Also, you might consider closing your door, if you have one, when you need to concentrate.

When someone unexpectedly drops in, stand up to talk. Don't invite your visitor to be seated unless you have the time. Usually, when you stand, your visitor will also stand. This should shorten the length of the visit. If this doesn't work, be honest and say something like, "Thanks for dropping in. You'll have to excuse me now, because I need to get this project finished."

Waiting

We all spend too much time waiting—for appointments, for meetings to begin, for others to complete something, for airplanes, and as we commute. Opportunities exist to make better use of all this waiting time.

Waiting time need not be *wasted* time. Two approaches will help: First, don't spend an unreasonable amount of time waiting for others with whom you have appointments. If you go to someone's office and aren't received promptly, leave word with a secretary to call you when your party is ready and return to your office.

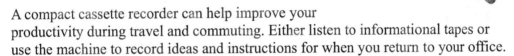

Second, make productive use of waiting time. For example, read your mail (including trade and professional journals), carry a pad and pencil to develop plans or write letters, or carry a file of low-priority items to complete.

A compact cassette recorder can help improve your productivity during travel and commuting. Either listen to informational tapes or use the machine to record ideas and instructions for when you return to your office.

Meetings

Time wasted in meetings comes from two sources: the meetings you call and the meetings you attend.

When you call a meeting, plan what you want to accomplish. Keep attendees to a minimum number of appropriate people. Briefly explain your agenda and move directly to the purpose of the meeting. Establish a time limit. Keep the discussion on track by periodically summarizing where you are. When the business has been completed, assign responsibilities, and establish follow-up dates to convert decisions to action; then adjourn the meeting.

A common time-waster is the "regular staff meeting." Two suggestions can make significant improvements. First, set an agenda by asking, "What do we have to talk about today?" If more material is generated than can be handled in the available time, prioritize the list. If nothing significant is offered, adjourn the meeting. A second suggestion is to eliminate any discussion that involves only two participants. These should be handled as one-to-one sessions.

Before you attend someone else's meeting, make sure it's necessary for you to be there. If it is, arrive on time and be prepared to participate in the discussion. Avoid taking the discussion off track or prolonging it. Work to make the meeting productive. Add any follow-up items to your list of things to do, within appropriate priority designation.

Crises

Many people believe crises are unavoidable. That's only partly true. Unexpected events do occur, and some must be handled then and there. Many crises, however, are recurring events brought on by something that either was or wasn't done. When you delay something that needs doing, you're helping to create a future crisis.

A starting point to reduce future crises is to review past ones. Are there patterns? Often you can develop a response to recurring problems. For example, if there has been a regular breakdown of a particular piece of machinery, you can replace it now or have a standby available for the next time it breaks down.

Another way to reduce crises is by planning for contingencies. Identify the key elements of a project. Then think through these three questions so that you'll be ready if a crisis occurs:

▶ What's likely to go wrong?

▶ When will I know about it?

▶ What will I do about it?

Some crises are beyond your control. For example, you may have unrealistic deadlines laid on you, priorities may be changed at the last minute, people may make mistakes, or machines may break down. When this happens, take a deep breath and relax for a few minutes. Think through what needs to be done and consider the alternatives. Then approach the situation in an orderly, methodical way. You don't want to precipitate a second crisis by the way you handle the first one.

DEALING WITH TIME-WASTERS

Now that you've read about time-wasters and how to deal with them, take a few minutes to look at your own situation. List as many time-wasters you've experienced as you can.

List of Time-Wasters

Self-Generated	Environmental

From your list of time-wasters, select the three most serious. What are they? How much time do they consume? What causes them?

_____

_____

_____

List possible ways to reduce the impact of these time-wasters.

_____

_____

_____

When Things Go Wrong

There will be times when nothing you do prevents the worst from happening. If a deadline is missed, here are some various solutions you can use to try to get back on track.

1. **Renegotiate**: The simplest action when you can't make a deadline is to renegotiate the due date. Perhaps there's enough flexibility that a day or two longer doesn't really matter.

2. **Recover Lost Time during Later Steps**: If, in the early stages of a project, a step takes longer than planned, reexamine time allocations for the remaining steps. Perhaps other time can be saved so the overall time for the project doesn't increase.

3. **Narrow the Scope of the Project**: Once underway, you may find it will take longer than planned to accomplish everything you planned. When time is critical, you may have to eliminate some nonessential things to meet a deadline.

4. **Deploy More Resources**: You may need to put more people or machines on the project. This option clearly increases cost, so it represents a decision that weighs the increased cost against the importance of the deadline.

5. **Accept Substitutions**: When a needed item isn't available, you may be able to substitute a comparable item to meet your deadline.

6. **Seek Alternative Sources**: When a supplier you're depending upon can't deliver within your timeframe, look for other suppliers who can. (You may choose to pursue other sources before accepting substitutions.)

7. **Accept Partial Delivery**: Sometimes a supplier can't deliver an entire order but can deliver the amount you need to get you past a critical point. After that, the remainder of the order can be delivered to everyone's satisfaction.

8. **Offer Incentives**: Incentives can be written into agreements or can go beyond the terms of an agreement to get someone you're depending on to put forth extra effort. It might be a bonus clause in a contract for on-time delivery, a penalty clause for late delivery, or simply buying someone lunch.

9. **Demand Compliance**: Sometimes it's necessary to stand up for your rights and demand delivery according to the agreement. Occasionally, an appeal to a higher authority will produce the desired results.

CASE STUDY: The Program Really Works

I've always admired how Bill does so much without seeming rushed. He always seems to have plenty of time when we talk. I know for a fact he rarely takes work home with him. I finally decided to ask Bill the secrets of his time management.

He began by saying he once had a real time management problem. Because of it, he looked for ways to make better use of time. He read books on the subject and put some of their ideas into practice. Bill explained that the most important lesson he learned was to adapt techniques to his individual situation. He explained the following four basic concepts as keys to his success:

First, and most important, Bill said, he always looks ahead. He lists the goals he's working toward and has a plan to get there. He said he's learned to anticipate when things are due without waiting to be asked. As an example, budgets are due the second quarter every year. Bill doesn't wait until he receives a memo requesting his budget; rather, he works it into his schedule.

Second, he establishes priorities. There's always more to do than the time to complete it. Occasionally, this may mean foregoing something he'd like to do in favor of something that has to be done. When setting priorities, Bill said he takes into account his management's wishes as well as his own judgment.

Third, Bill indicated, he learned not to try to do everything himself. He relies on his staff. Bill knows the people he can depend on and lets them do their jobs. He also trains others until he can rely on them.

Finally, he said, use only those techniques that help you. For example, he said he doesn't make a "things to do" list most days, because often his days are routine. However, when things begin to pile up, he always makes a list and starts at the top.

CONTINUED

According to Bill, that's it. Four basic ideas to help get better control over time:

1. Know your calendar

2. Prioritize demands on your time

3. Utilize the skills of others

4. Use techniques that help your unique situation

Case Study Questions

1. Do you think Bill's superiors see him as a good manager, and why?

   _____

   _____

   _____

2. How do you think Bill's staff feel about working for him, and why?

   _____

   _____

   _____

3. What did you learn from Bill's approach that could help you?

   _____

   _____

   _____

Part Summary

In this part, you learned that one's own **disorganization**, **procrastination**, and the desire to fulfill **personal needs** can lead to wasted time. You also learned that one's environment can generate **phone calls**, **mail**, **email**, **surfing**, **visitors**, **waiting**, **meetings**, and **crises**—all of which can lead to wasted time.

Time-Saving Tips
for Travelers

"He who would travel happily must travel light."

–Antoine de Saint-Exupery

In this part:

- ▶ Plan Your Travel Wisely
- ▶ Save Time at Your Hotel
- ▶ Put Your Travel Plans in Writing

Plan Your Travel Wisely

Is This Trip Necessary?

Business travel can consume a great deal of time. Because of this, it presents opportunities to save time by examining current habits and finding better ways. Some of these tips will also be helpful for personal travel.

Before booking your flight, make sure the trip is necessary. Some options to consider are: Can you handle it by mail or telephone? Can the person you plan to visit come see you? Can someone else go in your place? When you consider these options, you may find you can save time simply by *not* making the trip.

If you must make the trip, carefully plan the details. Start by writing your objectives. (What do you hope to accomplish?) Then, make an agenda for the meeting that will lead to achieving your objectives. Next, make a specific appointment with the person or people you plan to visit. Follow up with a written confirmation of the appointment and a copy of your agenda. Then, upon arrival at your destination, reconfirm your appointment by telephone.

If you have several appointments, plan your schedule to minimize travel distance between them. And, be sure to leave enough time to get from one meeting to the next. You can't always depend on finding a taxi or a parking space.

Alternatives to Travel

Teleconference: Teleconferencing, works well for simple information sharing and straightforward decision-making that require no visual presentation. It isn't a suitable venue for discussing more complicated matters. Also, teleconferencing isn't a desirable way either to begin or to further important relationships. However, given its limitations, it still can accomplish a lot and save considerable costs.

Videoconference: Videoconferencing has the advantage of allowing people to see one another as they talk. With the right equipment, videoconferencing can be very effective in transmitting information, and helps communication by allowing people to see one another as they interact.

Computer Conference: With the ability to communicate inexpensively, in real time, people are using computers and the Internet to bring geographically dispersed people together for information sharing, collaboration, and problem solving.

Choose the Best Mode of Travel

If your destination is 200 miles or less from your home base, consider driving. It will probably save you time when you consider the time spent in getting to the airport, parking your car, flying to your destination, and getting a taxi or rental car to get to your appointment. If you don't have a company car, consider renting one for the trip rather than using your personal car.

Another option often overlooked is to travel by train. There's excellent train service in many parts of the world, and you typically arrive in the central business district of a city, eliminating a long taxi or rental car trip into town from the airport.

If you have a company travel department or a contract travel agent, you'll be expected to make your arrangements through them. However, if these services aren't available, you can work through the travel agent of your choice or call airlines and hotels directly on toll-free reservation phone lines or use online booking services. Here are some time-saving tips when booking air travel.

▶ Try to book a direct, nonstop flight. Not only will your in-flight time be less, but you'll reduce the chances of delayed departures.

▶ Use e-ticketing and print boarding passes on line. This eliminates waiting in line at the airport for a seat assignment.

▶ Get information on flights that are both earlier and later than your scheduled departure. Then, if your plans change or your flight is delayed or canceled, you'll know what options are available.

▶ Ask for the on-time ratings of flights you're considering. This figure is readily available and tells you the percentage of time the flight has arrived on schedule during the past two months.

▶ Avoid Friday travel whenever possible. This is the industry's busiest day during a typical week.

▶ Avoid departures between 6:30 A.M. and 10:00 A.M., if possible. Mid-afternoons are the slowest times.

If you or someone in your office must handle your travel arrangements, several websites let you use your personal computer and modem to book flights, hotels, and car rentals at the best available prices. You can handle everything via your computer (including meal choice and seat assignment) and either have tickets mailed to you or obtain an e-ticket on line that you can print.

Make the Most of Travel Time

The best way to save time at check-in is to bypass the process as much as possible. Choose an airline that lets you print your boarding pass ahead of time. Don't check bags. This allows you to go directly to security and skip the lines at the counter.

Plan your wardrobe so that you can get by with carryon luggage only. Since most airlines have a restriction of two carryon items, the typical garment bag, briefcase, and suitcase present a challenge. One option is to carry a small portfolio rather than a briefcase and put it either in your suitcase or in a side pocket of your garment bag. Or you can consolidate your garment bag and suitcase.

If you must have more luggage than you can carry on, use curbside check-in. Because of the potential for lost luggage, always carry the minimum of toiletries and personal items with you with due attention to security screening requirements.

Waiting and In-Flight Time: You can recognize seasoned business travelers. They get through security in a flash because, when they step up to the metal detector, their shoes, belt, watch, phone, pens, coins, and jacket are already in the bin on the screener's conveyor belt. They know the FAA rules on what can be carried on, so they never get stopped for nail clippers or shampoo. Their laptops are out of the case and open in a separate bin, and they watch to make sure everything goes through before they step through the detector.

Then, before and after boarding the airplane, they make full use of their time. Their laptops are equipped with wireless adapters to take advantage of the wi-fi available in many airports and increasingly on planes as well. If they bring reading material, it's confined to books or magazines—no bulky files or long reports.

A smartphone offers a great deal of versatility. You can send and receive calls, texts, and email, or surf the Internet. Other available applications include a camera, maps, calendar, and weather updates— everything you need to stay in touch.

Listening to recordings of business books or other training material can be much more rewarding than listening to airline music or watching a movie.

Getting to and from the Airport: In most cities, you can travel to and from the airport by private car, taxi, bus, limousine, or rental car. Many people choose to drive their own cars in their home cities. This may be the best choice; but consider the convenience of parking at both your workplace and the airport. Also consider the availability of other modes of transportation to get you either to your home or to your workplace when you return. You may find another choice would save you time.

When you arrive at your destination, limousine service is the most convenient. The driver will be waiting for you, help you with your luggage, and deliver you to your hotel. Taxi service can also be convenient, but there may be a considerable wait at busy airports. Bus and van services usually involve a delay as you must wait for the van to fill up or the bus to operate on a schedule.

Getting around Town: All of these choices leave you without transportation after you've been dropped at your hotel. You must either walk or rely on taxi service for local travel. A rental car is more convenient if your trip calls for much local travel. To save time at the car rental counter, have a confirmed reservation. Most rental companies  gather and store in their computer all the information they need. With this information on file and a confirmed reservation, you can bypass the check-in counter and go directly to pick up your car. When you return, use the express return system to avoid waiting in line.

Save Time at Your Hotel

Most major hotel chains offer extra services geared to the business traveler. Take advantage of these services plus the following additional ideas to save time:

▶ Find the most convenient hotel. Ask the person you're visiting for suggestions, or have your travel agent check the hotels near the address you'll be visiting. If several people are flying in for a meeting, consider booking accommodations for everyone at an airport hotel.

▶ Confirm your reservation with a credit card and get a confirmation number in writing or make a note of it over the phone.

▶ Book your room on the executive floor if your frequent traveler program membership permits, if you have upgrade coupons, or if your travel budget can handle it. The additional amenities often include newspapers, light breakfasts, extra service people, and use of office equipment such as fax machines and Internet access.

▶ Streamline your checkout by calling up your bill on the television screen and reviewing it for accuracy. At most hotels, you receive a copy of your bill under the door on the morning of your departure. If so, you simply drop off your key on the way out. Checking your bill the night before helps ensure that everything is in order.

THINK ABOUT IT

What ideas presented here can save you time on your next hotel stay?

_____

_____

_____

List other ideas not mentioned that you've found helpful.

_____

_____

_____

Put Your Travel Plans in Writing

After all arrangements have been made, write up an itinerary of your trip. Include the names of people you'll be visiting with their addresses, phone and fax numbers, and email addresses. Include the date and time of each appointment. Show the date and time of departure and arrival along with flight or train numbers. Also, show the name, address, and telephone number of the hotel where you'll be staying along with your confirmation number.

This information should be emailed or given to family members, office staff, and anyone else who might need to contact you for business or personal reasons. (It's also helpful to take a copy with you.)

YOUR ITINERARY

Write an itinerary for your next trip:

_____

_____

_____

_____

_____

_____

_____

_____

_____

_____

_____

_____

_____

Traveler's Tips

▶ Be sure each trip is truly necessary.

▶ Take written objectives and an agenda.

▶ Confirm your appointment in advance.

▶ Choose the best mode of travel.

▶ Book the most direct flight.

▶ Avoid Friday travel.

▶ Avoid early morning travel.

▶ Print tickets and boarding passes in advance.

▶ Know the flights before and after yours.

▶ Carry on all of your luggage.

▶ Arrange the best ground transportation.

▶ Book the most convenient hotel.

▶ Take sufficient work to stay busy.

▶ Take any equipment you may need.

▶ Advise everyone of your travel plans.

Part Summary

In this part, you learned to examine planned trips to determine if they're truly **necessary**. Then, you learned about **alternatives** to travel. You learned how to determine the **best mode** of travel, and how to make the most of your **travel time**. You learned how to save time at your **hotel**. Finally, you learned to put your travel **plans in writing**, both for your own benefit and for that of others.

82

Applying What
You've Learned

❝ *Success is not for the timid. It is for those who seek guidance, make decisions, and take decisive action.*❞

–Jose Silva

In this part:

▶ Apply Time Management Principles

▶ Keep a Daily Time Log

▶ Analyze Your Use of Time

▶ Plan for Improved Time Utilization

▶ Follow Up on Your Progress

Apply Time Management Principles

This section contains worksheets to help you apply time management principles and techniques to your own situation. To complete this section, you need to do the following:

1 **Gather Data:** For one week, keep a daily time log similar to the one shown on page 101. This will provide accurate information to help you improve your use of time. Be honest—and attentive—to detail.

2 **Analyze Your Use of Time:** Working with the data gathered, analyze your current use of time. List opportunities for improvement.

3 **Develop Action Plans:** From your analysis, develop specific action plans to bring about the desired improvement in your use of time.

4 **Follow-Up:** Six weeks after beginning your time management improvement effort, complete the Progress Survey at the end of Part 5 to assess your progress, and determine what work still needs to be done.

Keep a Daily Time Log

▶ Select a typical week. Avoid weeks with vacation, sick leave, personal leave, holidays, etc.

▶ Record activities at least every half hour. Be specific. For example, identify visitors and record the duration and topics of conversations.

▶ Write a comment on each activity. Did something take longer than usual? Why? Were you interrupted?

▶ At the end of the day, note whether this day was typical, busier than usual, or less busy than usual. Add up time spent on various major activities (meetings, visitors, telephoning, mail, etc.), and show totals along with other comments at the bottom of the Daily Time Log.

Daily Time Log

Day of Week: M T W T F

Time	Activity	Comments
7:00		
7:30		
8:00		
8:30		
9:00		
9:30		
10:00		
10:30		
11:00		
11:30		
12:00		
12:30		
1:00		
1:30		
2:00		
2:30		
3:00		
3:30		
4:00		
4:30		
5:00		
5:30		

Was this day ❑ Typical? Comments: _____

❑ More busy? _____

❑ Less busy? _____

Photocopy this form for each day of the week.

Analyze Your Use of Time

Using your time log as a basis, draw conclusions and record your responses to the following questions:

TIME ANALYZER

1. Which part of each day was most productive? Which was least productive?

   _____

2. What are the recurring patterns of inefficiency (e.g., waiting, searching, interruptions)?

   _____

3. What do you do that may not be necessary?

   _____

4. What do you do that may be inappropriate?

   _____

5. Where are your opportunities for increased efficiency?

   _____

   _____

6. On what occasions do you allow enjoyment to override a priority task?

   _____

7. Which activities don't contribute to achieving one of your objectives? How can you change this?

   _____

   _____

8. On average, what percentage of work time are you productive? _____

9. What's your honest reaction to this figure?

   _____

   _____

Plan for Improved Time Utilization

Take five steps to make the best use of your available time.

1. State your time improvement objective.

Be specific in terms of both how much time you hope to free up in your weekly schedule and the target date by which you hope to accomplish it.

_____

_____

_____

2. Identify your areas of opportunity.

Be specific in what tasks might be eliminated or reassigned. What time-wasters can be eliminated or reduced? What planning needs to be done?

	Opportunity	Estimated Time Savings
1.	_____	_____
2.	_____	_____
3.	_____	_____
4.	_____	_____
5.	_____	_____
6.	_____	_____
7.	_____	_____
8.	_____	_____
9.	_____	_____
10.	_____	_____

3. Select those opportunities you plan to pursue.

Add up the anticipated time savings and compare it with your targeted time savings. (Space is provided to plan three opportunities. If you have more, photocopy as many additional pages as you need.)

Opportunity No. 1: _____

_____

_____

Action Steps	Target Dates
_____	_____
_____	_____
_____	_____
_____	_____
_____	_____
_____	_____
_____	_____

Opportunity No. 2: _____

_____

_____

Action Steps	Target Dates
_____	_____
_____	_____
_____	_____
_____	_____
_____	_____
_____	_____
_____	_____

Opportunity No. 3: _____

_____

_____

Action Steps	**Target Dates**
_____	_____
_____	_____
_____	_____
_____	_____
_____	_____
_____	_____
_____	_____

4. List others who need to be involved when implementing your changes.

This should include review and approval by your manager as well as the agreement and cooperation of those who may assume part of your duties and responsibilities.

Name	**Position**
_____	_____
_____	_____
_____	_____
_____	_____
_____	_____
_____	_____
_____	_____

5. Follow up in 30 days.

Review your progress and repeat any steps that haven't provided the results you anticipated.

Summarize your progress:

_____

_____

_____

_____

_____

What has interfered with your progress?

_____

_____

_____

_____

_____

How can you overcome these problems?

_____

_____

_____

_____

_____

Follow Up on Your Progress

Six weeks after beginning your time management improvement effort, complete the following survey. It will show where you're doing well and where you still need to devote attention.

PROGRESS SURVEY

Answer each of the following questions by writing the number of your response in the blanks on the left.

1 = Yes or Always   2 = Usually   3 = Sometimes   4 = Rarely
5 = Never or No   NA = Not Applicable

_____ 1. Do you have a clearly defined list of written objectives?

_____ 2. Do you plan and schedule your time on a weekly and daily basis?

_____ 3. Can you find large blocks of uninterrupted time when you need to?

_____ 4. Have you reduced or eliminated recurring crises from your job?

_____ 5. Do you refuse to answer the phone when engaged in important conversations or activities?

_____ 6. Do you use travel and waiting time productively?

_____ 7. Do you delegate as much as possible?

_____ 8. Do you prevent your staff from delegating their tasks and decision making to you?

_____ 9. Do you take time each day to think about what you're doing relative to what you're trying to accomplish?

_____ 10. Have you eliminated any time-wasters during the past week?

_____ 11. Do you feel in control of your time?

_____ 12. Are your desk and office well-organized and free of clutter?

CONTINUED

94

CONTINUED

_____ 13. Have you reduced or eliminated time wasted in meetings?

_____ 14. Have you conquered your tendency to procrastinate?

_____ 15. Do you carry out work on the basis of your priorities?

_____ 16. Do you resist the temptation to get overly involved in nonproductive activities?

_____ 17. Do you control your schedule so that others don't waste time waiting for you?

_____ 18. Do you meet your deadlines?

_____ 19. Can you identify the critical few tasks that account for the majority of your results?

_____ 20. Are you better organized and accomplishing more than you were six weeks ago?

_____ 21. Have you been able to reduce the amount of time you spend on routine paperwork?

_____ 22. Do you effectively control interruptions and drop-in visitors?

_____ 23. Have you mastered the ability to say "No" whenever you should?

_____ 24. Do you stay current with your most important reading?

_____ 25. Did you leave enough time for yourself (recreation, study, community service, family)?

_____ **TOTAL**

Add the points assigned to each item. The lower your score, the better. Look particularly at items you rated 4 or 5. These represent challenges for further development.

This survey should be taken quarterly as old habits have a way of recurring.

Time Management

Conclusion

Congratulations on completing this program. We hope it was an effective use of your time!

Nearly everyone has the potential to save five to 10 hours a week. To do so requires discipline and a commitment to the basic principles in this book.

In review, you need to identify the portion of time over which you have control. Then develop procedures for repetitive operations and make use of available technology. You should concentrate on high-payoff activities.

Also, identify and make best use of prime time—your personal energy cycle. Use prime time to handle work requiring concentration. If possible, arrange for a quiet period to match your prime time when there are pressing matters.

Next, establish quarterly objectives and construct plans to accomplish them. Maintain some flexibility to respond to unexpected events. Prioritize the action steps required to achieve your objectives.

Analyze your use of time. Keep a time log for a typical week and then examine your activities using the tests of necessity, appropriateness, and efficiency. From this examination will come the essential elements of your job so you can isolate time-wasters and deal with them.

Finally, remember that the ideas in this book must be adapted to fit your unique situation. Modify the worksheets if necessary, develop your own personal file system, utilize electronic equipment available to you, and use the planning techniques when appropriate. Don't let the use of forms and procedures distract you from doing your job.

Keep this program handy for reference. To check your progress, make a note to review the book again in three months.

Good luck!

Part Summary

In this part, you learned to apply **time management principles** by keeping a **daily time log**. Next, you learned how to **analyze** your use of time. Then you learned how to **plan** for improved time utilization. Finally, you learned how **to follow up** on your progress.

AX1424624908
ISBN-13 978-1-4246-2490-4
ISBN-10 1-4246-2490-8